Design

Also by Theresa Burns

Two Train Town (chapbook)

Design

Theresa Burns

Terrapin Books

Terrapin Books
4 Midvale Avenue
West Caldwell, NJ 07006

www.terrapinbooks.com

ISBN: 978-1-947896-53-6
Library of Congress Control Number: 2021953399

First Edition

Cover art by Scott Pilutik
"Theodore's Gift," 2021

For Marie and Evan and Gregory

Contents

What hath that flower to do with being white
    —Robert Frost, "Design"

Green, how much I want you green.
Green wind. Green branches.
The ship on the sea
and the horse on the mountain.
        —Federico García Lorca, "Somnambule Ballad"

I.

Someone Threw Down a Wildflower Garden in an Empty Lot in Newark

And now, instead of staring at the weeds
and broken bottles from the train platform,
we're taking in a scene from a Monet.
Asters, cosmos, little yellow fists
of something. All random and confetti.
I'm half expecting a lady in a high-waist
dress and bonnet to appear on a diagonal
stroll through its splendor, pausing
with her parasol so we can selfie with her.
Maybe she'll hop aboard the light rail
to the Amtrak station, get off in D.C.,
step back into the painting she escaped.
Who was the genius who thought of this?
What meadow-in-a-can Samaritan
got sick of passing the four-acre eyesore
on the walk to work? Shook pity into blossom.
To whom do I write my thank you—
mayor, surveyor, county clerk, church lady?
Who marched down to city hall, begged
anyone who would listen?

In March, Cut Back

butterfly bush, oakleaf hydrangea

        before they have a chance to leaf,

says Barb, plant authority up the block.

        Take the knockout rose back three feet,

start it all from scratch before the April

        rains begin. Cut back brittle barberry,

actually get in the bed and hack that shrub

        you never loved but keep

because it adds something—red. Because every human

        tires of all that green   *(how much*

I want you green)   but how much to leave

        and not overshade the peonies?

Bosomy sun lovers, their shoots

        look parched and need a shower

—like me, now I've cleaved for hours

        in sudden warm, swatted

and swore through it. Cut back thorns.

        Pinch the bleeding heart with fingers so dirty

my eye oozes when touched. My arms lashed

        by witch hazel, first flower to open

I cut back to make more.

Marie Thérèse

We gave our daughter my name, but backwards.

Thérèse in the middle
for de Lisieux—"the Little Flower"—
who followed her sisters to the Carmelites,
served as handmaid to the older nuns
till she died of TB in her twenties.
Or *Teresa* de Ávila,
just as motherless, Spanish mystic, reformer.

Marie we moved in front for my aunt who lived to 94,
served us gold potatoes mashed by hand,
used real butter from a glass dish. A practical woman,
a realist. *Marie* for her father's aunt, from whom
comes the only silver we own.

My daughter is no martyr, no hard ass;
her faith is thin as a membrane, as my skin
when she puts her finger through me.
Lately she's an apparition, at nineteen so self-
possessed, her visits a rarity.

Marie for the smile at the end,
the sunny, solid thing she was to hold,
and is, when we can. Her favorite season
summer. Her favorite color yellow.

Design: 1

I don't believe in all
the same thing
but in repetition, yes,
surely, yes. A shaky faith
in the rule of three:

trinity, a flowering
shrub here, and here,
and there. Then

against the glowback
of the familiar, the odd
answer appears—

a single daffodil
or hyacinth's nub, middle
of midweek.

And in between—
          I don't believe

     I don't believe
—evergreen.

Picnic with Sister-in-Law
in Mount Auburn Cemetery

1.

We are not here for the dead.
Though we slow down
for the oldest stones

       wordless ones

sunk cockeyed
in their lumpy beds.

We carry a basket of bread
and fruit. We are here to not hear
the trucks from the road,
to get out of the way
            of all that.

To search for a spot.

2.

We arrive in time
for the fashion show of trees—

blousy and pink-chiffonned and butter-cupped,
    each skirt pinned

with Latin name—*prunus mume*,
        magnolia stellata—
A crowd forms on the path.

High in the tallest oak:
            a newborn owl,
visible only through spotting scope.

We peer through it,
see nothing at first.
        Then his eyes, the white cloak
of his head.

He is the finale,
the wedding dress.

3.

On the way to the car,
Patty tells me
        about the son she gave up
at nineteen.

In the paperwork
she named him Theodore—
                        God's gift—

How can she even begin
to search the world
for him?

4.

From a distance, one tree appears
            filled with resting goldfinches.

Only when we reach it
do we see
                    its yellow blooms.

Read its name: *magnolia goldfinch.*

My Student Who Works
in Her Parents' Flower Shop

is late again. But because she smiles
her gardenia smile
as she bustles in,

S's of basket straw still
in her hair,
I draw a flower by her name,
not an L.

She's taken a cab this time
from the Lower East Side.
So who can know the corners
she's had to cut
getting here—

a touch too much baby's breath
in the wedding bouquet,
the ledger twenty dollars short.

The day the forsythia breaks
open, I prop some
in water on my desk

because we are trying to name things
precisely. *The forsythia's out,*
I tell them, though I'm pretty sure
no one else would care.

Her paragraphs
are a bramble of fragments, odd
syntax. Yet she excels

at this kind of arriving—
dirt-glazed, unrepentant.
Gone in a few weeks.

All Souls' Day

I was fifty before I really
considered teeth.

At the Advanced Dental Clinic
on Prospect, silver pockets from childhood
are removed, newly enameled.
Everybody Loves Raymond floats on the set.

How appealing they feel when she applies
the fluoride, pasty and dry,
after the deep cleaning. When I leave,
my smile is sincere, rooted.

Outside, the ginkgo leaves lose
their grip and fall. Through a window,
a film of yellowing ivy.

Nine months and no one has visited
my father. The teeth are still there, but not the body.
Not a headstone, but a pillow of leaves.

Last Week of Winter

The way the trees keep one another alive
in times of distress, share sugars and fluids
from the taproot up through pith
and sapwood, heartwood, the inner bark,
branch out through capillary action
to the terminal buds that dot their crowns,
take in the same ions that I breathe, and the ones
on any fringe breathe; and not just food
but news—secrets, warnings, gossip, pulses,
static, comprehending that to love one is to love
the hum of chatter beneath, the valley lit
by fireflies, the hive, the well, the drinking in,
the yard last April, to hang on—by pulp,
by first light, green, by sinew.

Ordinary Time

Though it didn't feel like a choice—
I was given my walking papers
and told to walk fast—

there was beneficence in my exile.
Leaving with no need to clean up,
absolved of all apology.

Weeks passed. First sleep returned,
then the endings of dreams.
I rode my bike to the park,

ate lunch by myself. I looked up
old friends and watered those tough
plants on their last legs.

I did a little meditation
at night, seated on a hard chair
in lamplight. *Thank you,* I prayed.

I called it Ordinary Time,
when people gathered not to talk
about work, or how much

they spent on something.
I went to a gallery or a church,
and didn't think of how to sell

the experience. I savored
a basketball game's last seconds,
the gorgeous, spinning orb

that at the right time, in the right
place, wins it all. Or falls.

Shade Lovers

Five straight days of rain,
and the enormous hosta we moved out back

fills out, blue as a lung,
threatens to inhale the ghost ferns,

hellebore. Like something before history,
when insects grew as big as gulls,

and the world choked on its own
oxygen. Here, under the canopy,

among the creepers and water suckers,
we thrive. While out in front the full sun

singes. How the annuals there
exhaust me. Passersby,

all their needs and thirsts. Stay
and rest with me, here. Be morning,

partial, as I am to you,
who knows to turn your gaze to the side

and let me breathe.

II.

Design: 2

In a dream, my sister Adele
tells me she loves the wind.

You love the wind? I ask.
All these years. How did I not know?

I love the goldfinch and the river
birch. I love my sister.

Less than two years apart,
a miscarriage between us.

Yes, the wind. If you can't see it,
it can't be taken away.

Knights of Columbus

When my father totaled the white Volvo
leaving his own driveway,
the airbag bloomed

like a calla lily, sparing him
the stares of the gathering neighbors. The sky
was just turning apricot. A downy tapping
on the hide of a dogwood.

He'd gone out to find my mother, he told us.
She might have been wandering
again, knocking on
strangers' doors without her teeth,
though she hadn't walked
the length of the block in years.

Maybe they quarreled. Maybe he
threatened something and left—
then in the middle of it, forgot what he'd do
if he reached that place alone.
He woke with a scratch on his chin.

Let him think what he thinks, we know
why it happened.
The dinner in his honor that night. Monsignor himself
would make the toast. O Grand Knight!
O steadfast heart! They would bestow the purple raiment, heap
unbearable praise on him.

To the Woman Who Was My Therapist for a Decade

Two years in, I didn't so much walk
to her office as ache along the window boxes
of 10th Street, my shoes loose and flapping
in my hurry. I co-opted her haircut first,
the way her hand cut across her brow—a wing
when she was thinking. Soon the dancers
and courtesans in the Matisse prints flew
from her rooms to mine and hung there.
A pass on the Ram Dass and the Thurman.
But yes to Jung, to *Being and Nothingness*,
how she taught me to meditate for ten minutes
in a side chair and get results. The day
she asked the group to tea in her apartment,
I arrived early: the table perfectly set,
as if she'd been there from the beginning,
laying out the honey and rolls for me
before the sun and other planets could join us.
Her living room walls so yellow, a kind of source,
and in that instant it became my doctrine,
my ancestry. Can you see why I wept
the following week when she buzzed me in—
by her chair, a bunch of black-eyed Susans
from another patient? Just opening up,
petals that same shade of yellow, and those
dark centers that so imperfectly
set them off.

Rainy Day Sisters

How gently we spoke with each other
the first weeks after he died.
At the house, huddled in his bed together,
and later on the phone when we returned to our
other families. Each weekend in April:
rain and more rain. Gently we brought our mother
the photos, helped her glue and press
their bodies close again. She in his uniform and army cap,
she holding his black dog. And when our names
no longer came to her, but mixed
like the names of the first weak flowers in the yard,
when the filters were finally shot, she looked up
from her work. *There's just one thing I don't understand—*
how did I get so damn good looking?

Love Song Without Wheat

If you can't eat it, I won't
eat it, he says to my sister
when she tests positive
for celiac. Then they make
of themselves a small country
in North Jersey where wheat
will not grow, nor be bought,
nor be baked into bread
or cake, and in their solidarity
they will no longer miss it.
Already her spine has a comma
at its base where the bone
is brittling like candy: symptom
of the thing she has. Let others
savor what is soft and warm
from an oven, torn into.
Their arms full of heirlooms,
deep greens to be sautéed
for supper, rice. Two glasses
of wine before the washing up.

Passage from My Son's Memoir

The only pets we ever owned
were goldfish. They lived for 12 years
no matter how filthy the water.
Dad claimed to be allergic to all
other creatures, not just cats and dogs,
but hamsters, guinea pigs, snails.
Mom accused him of laying it on.
They were amicable with each other
but not physical. There were moments
of underemployment, but no one
went hungry, though I worried
at times if the meat on the sandwiches
he made was still good. My sister,
who was the stronger of us, accused me
of being dramatic. This was no *Glass
Castle,* she said, a book she had
not finished. One day we realized
we had no grandparents.
When we said family, we meant this.
The others, the many aunts and uncles,
tried each holiday to restore
their parents' presence with warm
reminiscences, familiar jokes.
This is when they began to seem old.
When my sister left for college,
the house grew vast and calm
like a sea, and I became a boat on it.
Then I left. Mom and Dad spent more

time with the aunts and uncles
at the family beach house, the tip
of the long peninsula, until those waters
too began to rise.

The Gift

Black, slight, and sphynx-like—
a cat named Evening. One of a pair

my sister brought home from California,
along with a male ginger, Hugo.

We couldn't leave them alone.
Hugo would pull himself into shapes—

a shoebox, a dessert swirl
with chin turned up for kissing.

Evening slept where it was warm,
away from our eyes.

How could they be siblings?
we wondered, continuing our adorations.

After my sister returned to college,
Evening developed anemia.

That last week we kept her
near a heater, fed her with an eye dropper—

liver chopped fine
by my mother, who hated cats,

smoothed with milk over a low flame.
I looked into Evening's eyes as if

she had a soul borne of suffering:
Saint Sebastian, the children in *Maryknoll*.

Christmas morning, my father tried
to sneak her out in a towel, and I saw her

for a second, stiff,
the dull matted hair of some feral animal.

Hugo went off his food a few days,
then resumed his antics. It was a new year.

In California, my sister grew beautiful—
tanner and blonder and more alive.

"Love of Fire"

—John Conahan, composer

I miss hearing my daughter sing
at concerts, inside cold churches. In the old
videos I play sometimes, when she was still
in high school. A long burgundy dress,
the shoulders a little tight. None of the usual
self-consciousness as her mouth forms
a perfect O, takes in the visible breath—
that's how bad the missing can get.
So bad I swear I hear her single thread
within the skein of voices, know it as the color
that runs into me. After the Javanese folk dance,
and Ticheli's "Earth Song," which makes me
wonder if they are bound to this world,
they sing the one that begins a quiet rumble
in the core, builds like a storm-lashed river,
and burns like the last star in a too small sky.

III.

The Amaryllis

Still clap-closed, still podded like hands
in prayer, the amaryllis Julie gave me for Christmas
is still unbloomed. A thorough weekly
watering, she suggests;
more sun. I look for a window
on the first floor where it streams
in strong, but there is none.

                      I need a room
like the one I'd find my mother
snoozing in, late afternoon
in my growing-up house, the sun a wall-length
heat lamp, fierce healer of aches,
eraser of worries, where for twenty minutes each day
she could close her eyes, and open,
and dream of anything but us.

Proportion

When I say that his black
        leather belt gleamed

through the loops on his hips—

are you thinking
that he used it on us?

He didn't.
On his six four frame
it held up his pants,

which grew looser
as he aged,

        the belt traveling

higher on the gut, almost
comical, a Stanley

and an Ollie of a father.
Even as he shrank, the belt
rose, kept pace.

        But on those
few occasions we came home

late, shoeless,
having played so long
on our dull block,

our feet filthy, numb—

did he hit us on the high

back of the head,
knock the hair

into our eyes, snap us
            aware of those

twilight dangers? Who remembers.

And if he did, it struck us
as nothing uncalled for,
            entirely in proportion

to the act—
    our forcing him to notice

what we almost
got away with.

Twenty-third Winter

Maybe it's a form of cabin fever, my husband's sudden
need to be so useful, so necessary,

my own usefulness feels used up, emptied with the cans
and bottles he never forgets

to drag to the curb on Tuesday nights. Always the one
to drive our daughter at dawn to the pool—

and lately bring her home as well. *Thought you were still asleep*
he'll say, waving a sack of oniony bagels

or cider donuts cheerfully by the neck. There's a well
opening in me that I can't see the bottom of.

It's like we're in high school again and he's winning
Most Popular. And how can you complain

when a man makes dinner most nights and exhibits
a passion for laundry? When she got older, my mother began

to claim things in our home—*my refrigerator,*
my couch—as if her dominion over them was the source

of her worth. Tonight, I am starting the soup early
so it fills the house, lasts for days. My pots, my bitter greens.

Green

Did I tell you I had a Vespa once?
Pretty color, something between a turquoise
and the kelly green of my mom's favorite
sweater. Dad got the bike cheap from Hattenfisk's farm
when they sold. Teddy and I spent that summer
fixing it up, took turns riding it to the lake,
the rally races, and a couple of times to this spot
right here. We decided we wouldn't live
a life like Mom and Dad's. We wanted apartments
in the city, working in an office with air
conditioning and a gourmet grocery next door,
like Teddy has now. The first time we got high
was here, clouds purplish at midday, and where
the grass line set against the next mountain
glowed lime, and we laughed our asses off,
thinking it was the weed making things
extra green and alien. Now I see it's that way
at dusk too, the horizon lit and even more
lemony flowers I can almost taste, though that tree
on the right seems somehow diminished.
I'm not so bothered by things
these days, I get how the world is sweet
but bitter at the same time and it's no one's
fault. I can't even remember what happened
to the Vespa, if Dad gave it away or Teddy sold it
before he moved out. What about you?
Did you ever lose track of something you once
loved? And how did you get anywhere
without it?

Child Craft, Vol 1

Nights she read
from it,
shared her beloveds—

her tired voice
graveling down,

her voice a well
that drew us
in and down

and echoed back
its limits,

the pages overlaid
with scribbles,
Spirographed

and bulls-eyed,
its dull orange spine
shattered

from using it
as home plate, as placemat,

as food. Still
the poems
thrived there,

the verses stained,
the pictures, like the world,

unambiguous—
clear blue
for children's eyes and sky,

red for cloaks,

and purple for the cow,
the lines assured us,
we'd rather see than be.

School Night

She entered the room the way a moose
comes onto a road. Startling, foreign.
It took a minute to get her bearings.
Things hung off her like a Christmas tree
in February: laundry she brought up
from the basement, sunglasses she almost stepped on,
a schoolbag someone left by the back door
and might still need at 11 o'clock at night.
If there were four or five of us lit
by the TV, she moved slowly,
weighed shutting it off
in the middle of a Hitchcock movie, or the lone
sex scene she inevitably walked in on.
Or she might stand in front of it in disgust
as if she'd never seen this invention—
God give me patience. But if

there were one or two of us
reading—it could be the funny papers
or a dirty novel we found at the local pool—
she suddenly became delicate,
and moved around us quietly as a doe, maybe
smoothing our hair as she passed,
as if this were the only thing that mattered, as if
the house wasn't falling apart around us
and the only reason for her existence
was to ask us in her sweetest
mother voice: *Do you have enough light?*

Ode to a Station Wagon

I was never more grateful, you graceful
Passat wagon, with two-toned leather seats
and *sweet* sound system we bought
in flusher times, than the day you broke down
when it was my turn to carpool,
and I had to ask the other kids' mother
if I could take her car to school,
and it would have to be that mother who is never
undone, who runs the impeccable
cookie drive, the midwinter Blues Buster
with perfect gusto, who descended her staircase
at 7 am, a bit surprised in her bathrobe, and tossed me
the keys to her minivan, which I had a little trouble
starting, but was soon humming down the block,
children resettled in the back, not apologizing
to them, not even turning to see the inscrutable
faces my kids wore those years we lived
below the poverty line, and every action or inaction
seen through that lens, that side eye
that followed us to school and back, to Macy's,
the dentist and the deli counter, not caring
to hash out why they weren't getting braces
or a drink with that. They got to class
just five minutes late, and the fix that night
was quick and cheap, and you bet I stopped
at the carwash after, had you sudsed and buffed
to your former brilliance, so that next
morning when those girls slid in your indigo
doors, their mother would forget the image
of me in her driveway, unable to remove
the key from her ignition, asking her to please
come down a second time to help.

For the Ladies at ShopRite Who
Warn Me I Can't Leave My Bag There

You need to carry it close,
they tell me, strapped to your shoulder
or hugged like a babe to your breast
lest it be snatched, ransacked, emptied
of all its worth, then dumped in the parking lot
like so much chopped meat. Neighbors,
middle-aged like me, who've learned
to be wary. *Don't you have any sense?*
their pursed eyes seem to ask,
baffled at my mindlessness. And they're right,
of course. How often have I left my faux
leather sac with the busted handle unzippered
in the child's seat, practically begging
some stranger to pinch it while I perused
the salad greens, sniffed the peaches?
Not so much a fool as a flake, an easy mark.
My Irish mother, the same. My father scolding her
as she left church, her bag spilling
its rosaries and tissues, its silver pieces—
she with the nine mouths to feed. I'd like to think
it was her generous soul that made her
leave it slack, unguarded, easy enough to help
ourselves to the odd fiver. Hadn't she invited us,
never giving us an allowance? Keeping us safe
from all we couldn't purchase.
                    What I want to ask as I pass by, our carts
heavy with tomatoes tender to the touch—
why spend your worry on the likes of me?
Mother able to afford

her reverie? Are there grown ones of your own
you can't protect, no matter how close you hold them?
No matter how many warnings?
May they heed them, those daydreamers,
those walking-down-the-street whistlers.

Aubade with Rare Bird

I love you like I love the sentence—
the way a verb loves its subject. Nothing I wouldn't do

for you, captain of my starship. I love you like the dead
languages I discover in our junk drawer. Searching

for a scrap to write on, I unearth your faded messages
among the pen caps and pizza coupons. O mysteries

of Lascaux! Sanskrit, Sumerian. I murmur your name
like old women in churches. I worship your irrelevance,

your occasional oversharing. When we fight, I pull up
weeds by the root, toss them in a heap

with the unforgiven. Every neighborhood bitch stops
so you can rub her good, pooch whisperer, jealous

of me. Harebrained and morning-breathed, I ache
for your paws on me before you make the coffee.

Plague times, I'd swap spit, give up my last clean
sheets for you. Anyone messes with you, I'll get up at dawn

and Alexander Hamilton them for you. Which makes me
a fool, it's true. I'd chew on hemlock if it would

spare you. Love, we're alive. It's May, there's a Canada
warbler at the feeder and I'll share him with you,

his necklace of black bone, his yellow eye, the high
chipped syllables he won't waste on us for long.

IV.

My Daughter Comes Home to Quarantine

Here we are, like roommates from opposite coasts
drinking in the first warm day of spring.

I know she'd rather I was the boy at school
she had just begun to know,

and how I envy the ache she must feel
across that wirelessness.

She couldn't hide her disappointment
at arriving two months early, re-entering

her old room like a nineties hit song
she felt no nostalgia for. And yes, I wonder

what passes between them at two in the morning,
shyly or eagerly, on phones.

What more could they have to say, the string of lights
over her bed still twinkling,

Lizzo or Drake playing faintly through the door. I think
of all the times I said, *You don't listen.*

All the times I said, *Love the one you're with.*
Circumstance has paired us—

girls' night to make dinner, to wash up,
to watch SVU reruns to see how Benson, loveless,

will figure this whole thing out,
get home in time to put her kid to bed.

Now the sun on our skin is a warm
amnesia. She tells me about a friend who wants it to be

the way it was before a boy left her,
then left her again. In other words, impossible.

Hair Story

The decades of office hair.
Cropped and bobbed, quarterly highlights.
Interview hair, designed to move up.
Then the long unraveling. Kids home
from college, half-hour-shower hair, to hide
acne, big ears. Hair to be snaked
from the drain, detangled, forgotten
to brush. Who cares? We don't go anywhere.
Acres of hair, bushels, a hectare.
Hair in the way. French twisted, scrunchied,
tied back with socks, teeth-gripped, braided
in thirds. Hair gaining on us, losing loft.
Sit in a kitchen chair while my husband L'Oreals
my hair. Hair in my food, in dreams going back
to high school, hair to my ass. Neil Young
swarmed in Central Park. Crazy Horse hair.
Broken guitar string. First love with his thick
mane out the car window, softest hair,
cut short at his wake. Hold back my hair, friend,
while I lose my guts. Hair I twirl like a girl
again.

The Tutor

The first time the boy came
his mother brought me tea—
fine British tea in a lavender tin. I'd never had a client bring me

a gift, and as we went upstairs
to work, I imagined how good
the tea would taste, with a sweet or slice of green apple.

In the room together,
instead of finishing his story,
the boy cried in a chair. Not for a minute or two, but for the whole hour,

and I sat beside him, my hands
in my lap like two dead fish.
His story recounted the time he hiked with friends in a Colorado

mountain pass. The others
walked ahead of him
through shimmering aspen. The boy fell on a branch, twisting his ankle,

but he wouldn't call out—
he didn't want to ruin
his friends' good time. A half hour passed before they returned

to find him, shouldered
him back to camp.
He knew his story needed to say how he was changed by this incident.

That is the part he couldn't write.
His description of the mountains,
though, contained some of the most sublime sentences I had ever read,

and I told him so. Then we sat and drank
the tea his mother had given me,
tea I served to him with a sweet because I knew he wouldn't ask.

Grizzly

In my cabin a pine knot bleeds its clear heart
and hardens, making me think rain has come through.

I still can't hike at dawn for what may come out at me.

When I look into your brown eyes, I see
the bear I am afraid of,

hungry, dragging everything it owns: leaves,
bone, teacup and tea ball. When I think of you at seven

waiting in pajamas for your father's flush
and arrival, I want to be the wilderness you thought of

at just that moment, before the hallway light landed on you,
then went out.

Women in Treatment

Why had I not noticed them
before? The women in treatment
on every block, it seems, leaving
the library, walking their dogs.
Once they hid themselves
beneath wigs, fashionable hats
in the city, or entered softly
in Birkenstocks and baseball caps,
stayed out of the way. Now they
show up, unannounced.
In offices, in waiting rooms,
in aisle seats with legs outstretched,
the women in treatment
flip the pages, reach the end,
bald, emboldened. One
outside a florist today arranges
lantana in time for evening
rush. A bright silk scarf
around her pale round head
calls attention to her Supermoon.
And one woman my own age,
in my own town, takes up a table
right in front. She nurses a chai latte
in a purple jacket, her hair
making its gentle comeback.

Design: 3

—after reading Patti Smith's M Train

In college the boys wanted
her ghost horse body.
The girls wanted to live
inside her boy body.

Her words we heard
as drug induced. This Catholic
girl from Jersey.

Today I drive the wide
boulevard in Rockaway—
    wide because its shoulder is the sea—

searching for her house
near me. I know it
from the book,

a sad little thing she bought
despite its sunken porch, leaky
roof, trashed garden.

Will she dream now
in gray-greens,
of weather stripping
and storm drains?

Of whole blocks
of houses on stilts?

I could walk her through
these canyons. Show her what few
originals survive.

Where forty years ago my uncle
dug out the cesspool
of our bungalow,

his freckled back bent to it,
another Winston
pointed at his mouth.

I search for her
the way I search for most things—
always more want
than design: the body

to keep working,
the fog to lift, the coolness
of the train ride

that delivers us to the water,
the taste of that salt.

The Language of Empty Storefronts

Did you know me when I brimmed
silver and turquoise? Fine cotton
and incense. The owner spoke Punjabi,
or hippie, burnished my tin ceiling
to a warmth unseen on these avenues.
Not long after, I held a dozen tables
at which whole families knelt to eat
from little bowls of *gomen,* scooped up
with warm *injera* once the Coptic prayer
of thanks was said. Then the Sneaker Shed.
My fresh white walls lined with Air Max
and Chuck Taylors, the pride I felt
when thrice-showered teenage boys
lingered there. (By then, they'd covered
my tin with immaculate foam, a meter
lower.) Don't believe the drab brown
dress of paper and packaging tape
they've draped me in. Don't listen
to the absence of clinking glasses. I am still
the language a violin speaks when taken
down from the wall of a music store.
The scent of sandalwood, notes of cardamom
as someone locks up for the night.

Teaching Whitman in the 21ˢᵗ Century

They weren't ready when I first brought him out, '04, '05 maybe.
Short hair was fashionable again. Even the college kids
clean shaven as stockbrokers, and here he was all bearded and louche,
holding their gaze from the yellowing flyleaf. The boys especially
squirmed in their seats when I told them he was gay, or at least bi,
and suddenly they understood stalking Lincoln through the streets
of the capital. Wandering like a dreamer into enemy territory.
The prose they liked okay, concerned mostly with War and Death,
which were safe. But wasn't he getting a little weird about the soldiers,
young men he nursed as they died alone under tents. He held
their hands like the children they were, penned their last words
to their mothers and fathers. My students grasped his outsized heart.
How they shrank, though, when we read the long poem, that
unleashing. How strained the room became as they went around,
mouthed their two run-on lines, then dropped their eyes
to their phones again. Song without apology, without shame.
At twenty, I cringed too: *Who is this guy?* So full of his selves,
himself larger than the world, himself in every beast and flea
and paramecium. Only when I got a little closer to the dirt,
my parents ready to nestle there for good, I came again to his long
lines lapping like tides coming in, receding, then advancing.
Around '09 or '10, I felt a shift like weather changing, and we read
the poem where he bends to kiss the enemy soldier on his cold
white lips. And not a single one of them giggled or muttered *gross*
though they had absolutely nothing to say about it, nothing
about any of the lines he had crossed, sentences he had
eradicated with that kiss. A couple years later I shut the door,
made them commit. We stood up and belted the lines, slingshot
them across the room, and when we got to the dirty parts,
kept going. When we finished, one of them muttered *sick*. But not
the kind of sick they meant a dozen years before. He meant sick
as in *awesome*, as in *epic*, as in *Who the hell is this guy?*

Desire

Gave out finally upon learning of the death
of Adam Schlesinger, lead singer
of Fountains of Wayne. The news shared
by my husband as he lay in bed
checking Facebook, me scanning
the medicine cabinet for a sleeping pill. How long
had it been the phone he regarded before sleep?
Desire had survived childrearing, unemployment,
bad mattresses, depression, and the fear
that one, if not both, had contracted some virus
while commuting to and from work.
The depression had centered around leaving
the city sixteen years before. Yet there were pleasures
available here that were absent in New York—
peonies, black-eyed Susans, coneflowers,
Asiatic lilies, and Japanese forest grass,
which didn't even have a flower. As the cones dried,
their seed heads attracted the American goldfinch,
whose flash of intense yellow had an effect
similar to a snort of cocaine during those years
on the West Side. There was also a band,
a distinctly Jersey band, whose sweetly plaintive
melodies made us both go quiet in the car.
Hearing the news in the bathroom made me stop
and notice my just-brushed teeth were numb,
my tongue cold. I returned to my side
of the bed, lay silent as he played one of their songs
on his phone. We'd been told not to touch
our faces. We did not touch each other's face.

Embarrassed by Orange

Without irony, he wears the paper crown
from Burger King,
allows me that crinkled pleasure,

still laughs
as dogs and cats in old cartoons
spin syrup-wise around a tree.

About orange
he is unabashed. Though it unseats me,
O clown color, secondary,
always the bridesmaid to purple

or red, the wild peach, screaming or juiced,

color of Cheez Whiz and chips, the ball
dribbled low.

And in our garden, that siren he and I planted, *Deciduous Azalea*—
so cheap and tall and tangerine,

it's dizzying. For two short weeks
in May she blares out there, outbrights the daylilies,
the Siberian irises.

V.

Brick City

Sorry, did I brush you?
Did I touch the soft

meadowland
above your elbow

by mistake?
Did I stroke you

on the train as I leaned
for what I needed?

Did I break you,
did it send us to our corners

into pieces, did I
knife you while the night outside

turned black the window,
turned our faces inside out?

Unbearable this nearness,
can you face me,

this approximation
of kinship, do you hate me,

to our corners you can
switch here, Brick City,

sorry, get hitched
here, sorry. Erase this

strangeness was there something
I missed here, sorry

did I break you
by mistake?

Jardin des Plantes, 1980

Sometimes I wanted to crawl into a cave myself
when I watched the unfortunate baboons
palming their mangos at the zoo across the street,
then trying for hours to lick the stick off themselves.
I felt sorry for them as I felt sorry for the birds
in their high windowless cells—what good all that
red iridescence, all that sky-pitched soar?—
but not as sorry as I felt for myself that spring.
Nineteen and alone, no dancing in *boîtes* along
la Huchette, no fine-boned boys walking me
back to my room where I kept a knife
and a hotplate and a penlight so I could open
the right door when I visited the bathroom late,
my hand along the wall when the timed light
timed out, the hallway that held the most amazing
smells, crêpe and sleeping animal, pissoir and coffee.

To the Professor I Lived With,
Whom My Mother Called Svengali

Because you introduced me to your friends
as a poet, I wanted to be a truck driver,
worm composter, game show host. Because you
encouraged me to work upstairs, lay bare the sins
of Reagan Doctrine, I longed to sleep late,
read your journal over lunch, make puns
bad enough to embarrass you at parties.
When you held forth in your sonorous professor
voice, invoking Derrida and Foucault among your
Filofaxing friends, I'd take out my scissor-
tongue and slice you into parallelograms,
half-truths that fought to become whole. Who's
deconstructed now, I thought, happy
and alone. I carried around a book back then,
The Pill vs. the Springhill Mine Disaster, read it dozens
of times, trying to assume Brautigan's casual
penetration of suffering and the smog
of love. Still, there was one poem about a woman
he thought could lose twenty pounds,
so even that house had to be burned down.
It was decades before I could call myself
without irony a poet, allow myself into that club
of steadfast bees, living flower to flower
for whatever sticks to us, or is carried by the wind
to seed the world.

The New Black

Because I wore an orange
sweater to the reading, possibly one

with flowers, and had my black
standard-issue MFA glasses

holstered for the moment
in a pocket of my mom jeans,

my poet friend apologized
to the emcee while introducing me,

hand at her throat, assured him
good naturedly that though

I lived in Jersey now, I did in fact
reside in Brooklyn once

and, despite appearances,
belonged among them, the ones

in black leather, black jeans,
Doc Martens, ombre hair, smoke

lenses, each one a small storm
gathering as he took the stage

to read, features illumined
from below, crepuscular,

and I wanted to shout, *Am I not
one of you, brother, confrère*—

though I've taken the train
to this dive, not the subway.

And the trees of the town I just left
were exploding like seltzer

bottles thrown down a stair.
What's more, I have a garden there,

and the craziest orange azalea
opened just last week,

its color the latest cheesy
devotion I wear on my sleeve.

Places I Never Went on Vacation

Had I married that investment banker Derek
my friend Nate introduced me to in the late eighties,
I might have already been to Turks and Caicos
or even Greece. I'd be wearing a lot of winter white
and having my nails done regularly in French tips.
Instead, I remember sitting across from him
at a really great restaurant in New York, the kind
of restaurant we were always going to back then
on the company credit card, and he told me
what he was looking for was a wife. *A wife and kids
and a dog* were his exact words. And for a second,
I thought it was an indirect proposal, something
we would laugh about one day with our kids and our dog
all piled together on our neutral couch. But soon
it became clear I was not this wife he was looking for,
and just as certainly I knew this would be our last
meal together, with appetizers and dessert,
and a wine he would carefully select without consulting
the price list. We would not be traveling to Greece
or Rome, places we had talked about days before,
and I would keep wearing what I always wore,
tee shirts and boyish tops with a collar, sandals that
could not hide my big feet. Ten years later,
I married a man who took me to good restaurants,
our favorite the little cantina off First Avenue,
where the smell of cilantro hit you at the front door.
We bought a house in an old part of Jersey, a place
I checked out with Nate, who lived there
for a while with Jenna, his beautiful wife. I recalled
their wedding, years earlier at her parents' estate,
the waitstaff and billiard room, and I'd thought at the time,

Man, Nate really stepped in shit. Only they're divorced
now, he told me. Jenna got fed up with the writing,
wouldn't let him see the kids, ultimately got
a restraining order. Tonight, I'm thinking about Nate
and Derek and the vacations I never went on.
Feeling not just thankful for the house we fixed up
and the garden, the two girls next door jumping
on their trampoline, letting out little happy yelps.
But a kind of heart-pounding, sweaty relief.

Design: 4

        and when I came back
it was like slipping on a glove,

smooth, of cool cotton,
and with each flinch

of finger I entertained again the unreached
and carelessly abandoned

endings, until I couldn't count,
if I had a hundred hands

couldn't number my failures.
But even this, I understood,

was beside the point
because the body itself kept breathing,

taking stock of its requisites,
its cells and circuitry

quietly repairing themselves,
its dumb, insistent heartbeat

the most intelligent thing in the room.

Evening Swim

Sometimes after
        I feel like I've drunk something.

               Not the mouthful

of chemical water I swallow
        on the flip turn,
              but an elixir that makes

my limbs longer,
        makes my lungs a city—
              lights on all night

in my rented body. I slip in
        as the sun calms down,

              as the deer emerge

to nibble the hosta.

        I can wait like a champ
            for a lane. I can read

till there's almost no one.

        A coach I once knew
            told his swimmers, *Leave it all*

in the pool. He meant save nothing
        for later—

                               burn it down.

It's Sunday
                in my small town and my smooth
                                strokes go mostly unnoticed.

Sometimes I stop to drink
                like a beautiful animal
                                whose eyes see a distant place

I can't.   I leave it all there.

For Tina, As I Turn 60

I think 50 is the new 30, and 70 is the new 50.
—Tina Turner

Golden mane you nodded like a bobble-
head on a potholed road

shimmering dress you wore
into your seventies
        shook like my grandma's lampshade fringe

the legs   powerful as railroad ties
        nailed to your black heels   the threat

as you strutted across the TV
when I was 13.   *Where's Ike?* I asked my sisters.

Why's his name first when it's all her?
They shook their heads as if they possessed

intelligence they couldn't share.
   Tonight the newest goddess on screen

leaves me hungry.
But you, Tina, chewed through

harmony, matching suits   through *nice*
        salvaged gravel and *rough*   held it

by the teeth for fifty years.   Could it be
that long since I danced on our coffee table

pretended because I could pretend

it was a cage   a pair of leggy tights
on my head so I could rave
and toss the length of them as I did The Swim?

By your math, Tina,
I'm somewhere between 30 and 50

                and that feels like an ocean—
all the birthing and bleeding and sinning

and forgiving still to come.   My shoulders broad.
My memory has legs and that

makes me
the mister   the queen of this river.

Letter to My Almost Former House

It's true, I'm getting ready to leave you.
You're big and cold and expensive, and like any old lover,

I've begun to badmouth you to friends.
Once you were the center of my expanded life,

full-skirted host to my largesse. Display case
for dead aunt breakfronts and thrift store taste.

A cool backyard of Japanese maple and pine,
four types of hydrangea, and family close by. *Come in, come in—*

I'd coo to neighbors, meter readers, college friends
out from the city. *Sorry it's a mess,* though I'd swept

through your rooms like a hurricane. Twice I held
Thanksgiving here, that deadly sin of pride,

and thirty chairs etched scars on your floors.
Now the dining room sits empty. The staircase quiet.

The gaudy bills pile up and the flooding
holds us under. Soon someone else will sit out back

on jasmine evenings, share a cigarette and two fingers
of good whiskey while the kids fall asleep, compare

your century-old body to a big bucket of cream.

Last Request

When I'm dying, I may pass
on a sumptuous meal, ask instead
to ride the bus down Fifth Avenue
on a day like this one. June sky
a Looney Tunes blue, the skins
of sycamores peeling to fresh.
I'll start in the nineties, where if I squint
I can be in the 16th arrondissement—
so many mansard roofs sluiced
with pigeon droppings, X-rays in trim
Chanel suits headed out for tea. Let me
ogle the Guggenheim again, imagine
the planets in Klee paintings
tracing ellipses on the hive walls.
In the row ahead: a black-pirate-
hatted woman, spitting image of Marianne
Moore, a good witch to have
near the end. Let our driver worry
about four o'clock traffic. And the wait
as we kneel for the wheelchaired
passenger to embark. Me, I'm in no hurry.
Make as many stops as you like. I love
these big dirty windows, the perfect
height of my perch. *Look Marianne,
no hands!* Only the one writing down
on an envelope—
                    Be an eye at the end,
not a brain, or a heart.
Just a muscle that records what it's seeing:
ginkgo, street lamp, line.

Acknowledgments

Grateful thanks to the editors of the following publications in which several of these poems first appeared, in some cases in slightly different versions:

America Magazine: "Knights of Columbus"

The Cortland Review: "Shade Lovers"

Journal of the American Medical Association (JAMA): "Love Song Without Wheat"

Journal of New Jersey Poets: "In March, Cut Back," "Teaching Whitman in the 21st Century"

Literary Mama: "Child Craft, Vol 1"

New Ohio Review: "Last Request," "Someone Threw Down a Wildflower Garden in an Empty Lot in Newark," "Women in Treatment"

The Night Heron Barks: "To the Professor I Lived With, Whom My Mother Called Svengali," "Twenty-third Winter"

Paterson Literary Review: "Green," "Places I Never Went on Vacation," "School Night"

Plume: "Letter to My Almost Former House"

Rust + Moth: "Design: 1"

The Same: "Grizzly"

SWWIM: "Jardin des Plantes, 1980"

2 Bridges Review: "Picnic with Sister-in-Law in Mt. Auburn Cemetery" *upstreet:* "Rainy Day Sisters"

West Trestle Review: "Aubade with Rare Bird"

"The Amaryllis" first appeared in *Pain & Renewal: A Poetry Anthology,* ed. Brian Geiger (Vita Brevis Press, 2019).

"The New Black" first appeared in *On the Verge: Poets of the Palisades III,* eds. Paul Nash and Denise La Neve (The Poets Press, 2020).

"All Soul's Day," "Brick City," "Knights of Columbus," "Ode to a Station Wagon," "Proportion," and "Rainy Day Sisters" appeared in the chapbook *Two Train Town* (Finishing Line Press, 2017).

"Green" was featured in the exhibition *Painted Poetry* at the West Caldwell Public Library in July 2018.

The seed of this book began in Sarah Lawrence's MFA program in poetry, so I want to thank the faculty and students from that time, in particular Thomas Lux, Vijay Seshadri, Marie Howe, Kate Knapp Johnson, Billy Collins, Suzanne Gardinier, Elaine Sexton, Michelle Valladares, Curtis Bauer, Kaye McDonough, Pat Rosal, Miles Coon, and Mary Alice Rocks.

Invaluable to me for the last dozen years has been the support of two regular poetry writing groups. Sally Bliumis-Dunn, Alison Jarvis, Judy Katz, and June Stein of The Riversides have shared insights on virtually every poem in this collection, pushing me to improve every one. June spent weeks over a pandemic summer helping me wrest an early draft of the manuscript into submittable shape. In New Jersey, The Lady Mechanics—Tina Kelley, Jessica de Koninck, Marcia LeBeau, Elinor Mattern, Helen

Mazarakis, and Carole Stone—have been my rock, their talent, consistency, and productivity keeping me honest and focused. Thanks also to the Sunday Poets—Broeck Blumberg, Lisa Bruckman, Laura Freedgood, Susanna Lee, Marilyn Mohr, Jennifer Poteet, Susanna Rich, Frank Rubino, Arthur Russell, and Lia di Stefano for their feedback on several of these poems. As the manuscript evolved, I received essential editorial input from Rosebud Ben-Oni, Baron Wormser, and Lynn Melnick.

I also want to thank several recent workshop teachers and friends who inspired or enhanced the poems that appear in *Design*, including Chas Carner, Stephanie Cawley, Barbara Daniels, Jennifer Franklin, Michael Lally, Nathan McClain, Christine Salvatore, Sean Singer, and BJ Ward. Thank you to Peter Murphy and his entire team for providing virtual spaces to keep poetry close during a challenging period.

Diane Lockward, my editor and publisher, has been a true collaborator throughout the process of bringing this book to the world. From her early encouragement on a not-quite-ready manuscript, to her patience while deciding on nuances of a cover, Diane has been the kind of attentive, tough-minded steward every author wants and needs. I appreciate her belief in *Design* every day.

I am grateful to Scott Pilutik, whose existence inspired the poem "Picnic with Sister-in-Law in Mt. Auburn Cemetery." Scott's gorgeous photo graces the cover of this book. Glenn Wright, the best graphic designer I know, shared his considerable skills in getting the cover just right. Thank you to Anne Wessel, who helps keep poetry alive for me throughout the year as we collaborate on Watershed Literary Events. And to Ethan Galvin at the Hoboken Public Library for giving me several opportunities to read and record my work for a wider audience.

Thank you to my family members, all of whom are woven deeply into these pages. To my late parents, and to my eight siblings who are truly my best friends—thank you for being so funny and interesting and inspiring. And finally, to my nearest family, Marie and Evan and Gregory, who put up with a lot over the years while I tried to get this thing right. You are my favorite poem, the one I couldn't do without, the one we're all still writing.

About the Author

Theresa Burns is the author of *Two Train Town*, a limited edition chapbook. Her poetry, reviews, and nonfiction have appeared in *The New York Times, Prairie Schooner, New Ohio Review, JAMA, The Cortland Review, The Night Heron Barks, Plume, SWWIM*, and elsewhere. She earned her MFA in poetry from Sarah Lawrence College. A long-time book editor in New York and Boston, she is the founder of the spoken-word series Watershed Literary Events. She teaches writing in and around New York and currently lives in South Orange, New Jersey. An earlier version of *Design* was a finalist for both the Barry Spacks Poetry Prize from Gunpowder Press and the Homebound Publications Poetry Prize for 2021. *Design* is her debut full-length collection.

www.theresaburns.org

CPSIA information can be obtained
at www.ICGtesting.com
Printed in the USA
BVHW050900220322
632082BV00002B/243